Darlings, Y...
Wonderful!

A comedy for women

DARLINGS, YOU WERE WONDERFUL!

First staged at the Shropshire Drama Festival in Pontesbury
Village Hall by Wellington Drama Club on 7th March, 1989, with
the following cast:

Vanessa	Beryl Edwards
Judy	Annie Savage
Irene	Alice Seal
Eve	Linda Wakeman
Liz	Anne Burnett
Lesley	Tevan Gandy

The play was directed by **Derek Lomas**

The action takes place in the dressing-room of a Little Theatre

Time—the present

AUTHOR'S NOTE

The author wishes to emphasise that if the ending of the play is to have its full impact the stage directions should be followed implicitly. The cast must continue to act until the final curtain

D.L.

DARLINGS, YOU WERE WONDERFUL!

The dressing-room of a Little Theatre

As it is below ground level there are no windows. There is a door UR *up to the stage and another* UL *leading to the toilets. The furniture consists of a make-up table along wall* R, *with a mirror surrounded by light bulbs (half of which are dead). On the table are an open make-up box and a grey wig on a block. There are chairs and stools, a costume rack on castors and a small convector heater against the back wall. Mounted on the wall over* UR *door is a loudspeaker cabinet. The main source of light is a 150 watt bulb in a green shade hanging* C. *On the floor is a threadbare carpet*

As houselights go down, classical Spanish guitar music is heard. Tabs open on a dark stage. After a few seconds stage lights come up and the music fades. Vanessa is seated DC, *reading—rather flicking through—a magazine. By the side of her chair is a large leather bag. She is wearing tight ski pants, red polo neck sweater and a white fur jacket draped over her shoulders. Her hair and make-up are immaculate. She is smoking*

After a few moments Judy enters briskly from the UL *door and passes behind the costume rack. She is dressed for her part, that of an elderly retainer in an aristocratic Spanish household of the mid-seventeenth-century, in a long-sleeved blouse buttoned to the neck and a long skirt, both in dark brown. She is Welsh*

Judy Just as I thought. There wasn't any.
Vanessa Sorry?
Judy Loo paper. Not a scrap.
Vanessa Oh. (*She turns a page*)
Judy It was the same last year. Had to dash to Tesco, caught them just before they closed. If I'd been five minutes later ... well, I don't know where we'd have been. (*Smugly*) So this year I brought my own. (*She moves to the table, picks up the aerosol and sprays the mirror*) I mean, it's not on, is it? (*She polishes the mirror vigorously*) The least you expect in a festival is a clean dressing-room. Look at this place. Filthy! They gave us the same

one last year. I told the committee we ought to complain, let them know how we feel ... but they wouldn't. (*She finishes polishing and stands back*) That's better. I mean, it's not as though we're Arabs.

Vanessa Arabs?

Judy Bedouin. They don't use it.

Vanessa Aerosols?

Judy Loo paper.

Vanessa They don't?

Judy No. They use sand. (*Pause*) Very fine sand.

Vanessa It would have to be.

Judy Then they only use their left hand to ... well, you know ... because they have to keep their right hand for eating and shaking hands. I saw it on the telly. Well, not it, not it exactly, but they had this man who'd spent all his life out there. Well, most of his life. A lot of it. Since he'd left school.

Vanessa Sounds fascinating. (*She blows a smoke ring*)

Judy No, it wasn't. I only watched it because they had sport on all the other channels and I'd forgotten to change my library books. The truth is I'm nervous and when I'm nervous I talk. Well, you must have noticed. I can't help myself. I talk or I have to be doing something.

Vanessa Like dashing out to Tesco for toilet paper?

Judy Or polishing. It helps take my mind off things. (*She glances over her shoulder to* UR *door, then draws her chair closer to Vanessa's*) It might seem disloyal, perhaps it is, but I've got to say it ... I think we might have chosen the wrong play.

Vanessa The wrong play?

Judy For the festival, yes. I mean it's a marvellous play, tremendously dramatic and ... and significant, but there aren't, well, many laughs in it, are there?

Vanessa Not intentionally, no.

Judy That's what I mean! People like a laugh. They like to leave the theatre feeling happy. There's not much chance of that after a play that ends with the heroine throwing herself down a well. (*Pause*) I know this is a festival and the important thing is to impress the adjudicator, not entertain the audience, but I think we might bore them.

Vanessa Have you told Madame how you feel?

Judy Irene?

Vanessa Well, have you?

Judy Lord, no!

Vanessa Why not?

Judy I couldn't.

Vanessa If you feel so strongly—

Judy I wouldn't dare! She's run this society from the year dot, ever since she left the Profession. You know she was with the Royal Shakespeare? She's acted with all the greats—John Gielgud, Peggy Ashcroft—

Vanessa Ellen Terry?

Judy No, I don't think so. You can't say to a woman of her experience in the theatre, "Excuse me, I think you've chosen the wrong play." She'd freeze you with a glance.

Vanessa Or turn you into a beetle then stamp on you. Sorry.

Judy No, whatever you think of Irene—and I'll admit she can be . . . well—

Vanessa Domineering?

Judy Demanding. You've not known her as long as I have, you being a comparative newcomer, see. She started this society; she's steered us to success and she's baled us out when it looked as if we were going under. She's an inspiration to us all. (*Pause*) It's just that this time, I think she's made a boo boo.

Vanessa A boo boo?

Judy A mistake.

Vanessa lets out a peel of laughter. She stands and crosses to the dressing-table where she stubs out her cigarette

Vanessa Judy, my love, she's laid an egg—and tonight the chickens are going to come home to roost. "The Well of Defilement" by Juan Ruiz de Aragon. By God, it's a farce!

Judy I thought it was a tragedy?

Vanessa The way we do it, it's a farce. Let's hope he's not watching.

Judy Who?

Vanessa Juan Ruiz de Aragon of course.

Judy But he's dead.

Vanessa I know he's dead.

Judy Then how—

Vanessa Oh, forget it.

Judy If he's dead then he can't be watching, can he? And if he was alive he'd be in Spain, wouldn't he? In Madrid or wherever. I mean, he'd hardly be likely to fly in all the way to (*Insert name of town where the play is being performed*) to see us perform his play in the BDL Festival, now would he? If we got to the finals, perhaps.

Vanessa Judy, we are not going anywhere. Except straight to the bottom.

Judy Sorry?

Vanessa Sunk without trace. We should have done "Goodnight, Mrs Puffin". You'd have made a wonderful Mrs Puffin.

Judy I played her in Porthcawl!

Vanessa There you are then.

Judy But we haven't any men. What can we do without men?

The loudspeaker crackles, followed by an ear-piercing whistle

My God!

Voice Testing. Testing.

Judy I wish he wouldn't do that.

Voice Good evening, ladies. We have forty minutes to lift off. I repeat, we have forty minutes to lift off. Message ends. Over and out.

More crackling, followed by silence

Judy The man's a fool! I could never understand what Irene saw in him. A woman like her could have had her pick. Aren't you going to change?

Vanessa All in good time.

Irene enters UR. She is in her early fifties, dark hair and eyes, pale complexion. She is wearing a simply cut dress in purple, her only ornamentation a large, antique ring on the middle finger of her left hand. She pauses in the doorway until satisfied her entrance has registered, then moves C

Irene Well, here we are. (*She smiles at Judy, ignores Vanessa*) Judith, let me see. Revolve, dear.

Judy revolves

Hm . . . yes. I don't care for the shoes.

Judy I wore them at the dress—

Irene And you're too pale. You're a servant, dear. A peasant. You need to be ruddier.

Judy Sorry?

Irene Ruddier. And you might black out a tooth. Resist the temptation to ape the gentry. Know your place.

Judy Yes. Ruddier, you said? (*She moves towards make-up table*) I'll do it now.

Irene It can wait. Would you be an angel and fly to the bar for a brandy? Just a dash of soda.

Judy No trouble. (*She moves to door* UR, *stops, turns back*) What about the audience?

Irene What about them?

Judy I'm in costume. I thought—

Irene Oh, they've hardly begun to arrive. If you look lively, no one will see you.

Judy Back in a tick.

Judy exits

Vanessa You've got her well trained.

Irene I'd hardly call it that.

Vanessa No? You snap your fingers and she jumps.

Irene glares at Vanessa, then moves US. She feels the heater

Irene This heater's cold. (*She moves back*) Judith is loyal. She's one of the original members of the Amazons. She may not be the best actress in the world—

Vanessa I had noticed. She can just about cross the stage without falling over the furniture.

Irene But she's loyal.

Vanessa In triumph and disaster, through fair weather and foul?

Pause

Irene You're a good actress, Vanessa.

Vanessa Why, thank you.

Irene You've a good voice and you know how to use it, a natural stage presence ... but I doubt if even your best friend, assuming you have one, would call you loyal.

Vanessa I take it this is leading to something?

Irene A clearing of the air.

Vanessa What exactly does that mean?

Irene If my husband wants to amuse himself with you, take you out to dinner, even take you with him on business trips to Dublin or Copenhagen ... well, as long as he's discreet, I'm prepared to look the other way.

Vanessa is about the protest, but Irene forestalls her

Don't bother to deny it. He has his interests and I have mine. He knows that just so long as he keeps me in the style to which I'm accustomed, then I'm prepared to keep him on a reasonably long leash. All I ask is that he doesn't mess on his own doorstep. You aren't the first bitch he's sniffed around and I don't suppose you'll be the last. (*Pause*) I suppose you're wondering why, knowing what I do, I haven't dropped you from the cast? I stopped caring a long time ago how Stephen amuses himself, although I've never ceased to wonder at his taste—or lack of it.

Vanessa Look here—

Irene The reason is I need you. Unfortunately, you're the only decent actress I've got. Eve and Liz are competent, but not much more; Lesley's a mixed-up kid with her emotional knickers in a twist and Judith ... well, Judith is Judith. Without you, we don't stand a chance. With you, we do. I came within an inch of winning the festival last year and this time I intend to bring it off.

Vanessa You're incredible! You walk in here and you call me ... you insult me, then calmly announce that you expect me to win the festival for you!

Irene Correct.

Vanessa I'm not going to.

Irene Oh, but you are.

Vanessa What do you think I am?

Irene We know what you are. I'm prepared to overlook it.

Vanessa If I refuse to go on that stage tonight, you can't make me.

Irene True.

Vanessa Too damn right it's true! And if I choose to walk out of this theatre, you can't stop me.

Irene No.

Vanessa So—

Irene You'll go out there tonight because you won't be able to help yourself. You've worked too hard, you've invested too much in this part to throw it away. (*Pause*) But if I should be wrong, if you do walk out on me, I promise you I'll leave my mark on you. I'll spoil your chances with my husband, or any man, for a long time to come.

Vanessa You wouldn't dare.

Irene Don't put money on it.

Judy bursts into the room

Judy One brandy and soda. (*She hands Irene the glass*)

Irene Thank you, Judith.

Judy Liz and Eve have just arrived. They had some trouble on the motorway. A flat tyre. Still, better late than never.

Irene What about Lesley?

Judy I haven't seen her.

Irene (*looking at her watch*) Thirty minutes to curtain. Stupid girl!

Judy Oh, she won't let you down.

Irene She'd better not. (*She puts glass on make-up table*) Excuse me.

Irene exits UR

Judy Oh dear! I wouldn't like to be in that young woman's shoes. How are you feeling?

Vanessa Oh shut up!

Vanessa storms into the toilet, slamming the door behind her

Judy Butterflies, I suppose.

The Lights fade. Guitar music for twenty seconds. Lights up

Eve, in costume, is sitting on stool at the table putting on her make-up. Judy is sitting US of her. Liz is at the costume rack. During the following conversation she changes into her costume

Eve ... and there we were, stuck on the hard shoulder. Couldn't get the wheel off, even after we'd jacked it up.

Judy How was that, then?

Eve Rusted solid, wasn't it? The wheel nuts. Couldn't move them. Then it started to rain.

Judy That must have been annoying.

Eve Annoying? I discovered words I didn't know I knew. Then ... seen the white?

Judy Number twenty? Here it is. (*She takes a make-up stick from box*)

Eve Thanks. Anyway, then this reticulated lorry pulls in behind us—

Liz Articulated.

Eve Thank you. This big wagon pulled in. The driver climbed down. All muscle and machismo, know what I mean? Anyway, he had 'em off in less than a minute.

Judy The wheel nuts?

Eve What did you think I meant? He changed the wheel.

Judy That was nice of him.

Eve Yeah. A real knight of the road.

Judy Did you give him anything?

Liz guffaws. Judy doesn't see the joke

Eve I did not! Mind you I was tempted to take him up on his invitation.

Judy Invitation?

Eve To climb into his cab and take off into the wide blue yonder . . . or wherever.

Liz Doncaster. He had a load of cat food for Sainsbury's. Did you know some of those big wagons have a bunk in the cab?

Eve See what I turned down? The chance of five hours of unbridled lust in some lay-by on the A1.

Liz Only five hours?

Eve I bore easily. (*She throws down the make-up stick*) That'll have to do. Now, powder . . . (*She powders herself off*) What's the time?

Judy Just after seven.

Judy Want the mirror, Liz?

Liz Thanks.

Liz has finished changing. She takes Eve's place at the table and starts to make up. Eve moves to heater and feels it

Eve This place is cold!

Judy Isn't it? I said to Vanessa we should have complained after last year.

Eve I've been in warmer bus shelters. Where is she?

Judy Vanessa?

Eve Our Lady of the Camellias, yeah.

Liz Miaow! (*She sees the brandy and takes a sip*)

Judy She's in the loo.

Liz How long's she been in there?

Judy Since just before you arrived. (*Pause*) Do you think she's all right?

Eve Why shouldn't she be?

Judy Well ... (*lowering her voice*) perhaps I shouldn't say this—

Eve Give.

Judy I went up to the bar to get Irene a brandy—

Liz is draining the glass. She pushes it out of sight behind the make-up box

—and when I came back the atmosphere was ... well, tense. Then Irene went upstairs to see if Lesley had arrived. I said something to the effect that I wouldn't like to be in her, Lesley's, shoes when she found her and then she, Vanessa, just ran in there.

Liz Curiouser and curiouser!

Eve Do you reckon they'd had a row?

Judy Oh, I think they must have had.

Eve You didn't listen?

Judy Listen?

Eve Behind the door—before you brought in Madame's brandy?

Judy Of course I didn't!

Eve You're too good for this world.

Liz So she's still in there?

Judy I just said so.

Liz Perhaps she's ended it all.

Eve Ended what?

Liz You know, this mortal coil. Perhaps she's, like, shuffled it off.

Judy looks blank

Snuffed it. The end. Finito.

Judy You don't mean—

Liz Exactly.

Judy But she couldn't have!

Eve As the man said, stranger things happen at sea.

Judy But this is a drama festival.

Liz So we're all at sea.

Eve Mind you, she's always been highly strung.

Liz That's because she's an artiste.

Eve Of course.

Liz I've got it!

Eve What?

Liz She's hanged herself.

Judy No!

Liz Even as we speak, her lifeless body is swinging from the lavatory cistern.

Eve Or—

Liz Yes?

Eve She could be bringing up a dodgy take-way.

Liz Indian or Chinese?

Eve Indian is favourite.

Liz You could be right. Yes, I can't see her topping herself without an audience.

Eve Not our Vanessa.

Liz No.

Judy You're joking!

Eve Sorry?

Judy You're joking. (*She looks from one to the other*) Aren't you?

Liz and Eve look at her, then at each other, then start to giggle. Their giggles give way to hysterical laughter

Judy You're mad! D'you know that? Mad!

The toilet door opens and Vanessa stalks out

She ignores the other three and as the door slams closed behind her crosses to the costume rack and begins to change. Liz and Eve are silent. After perhaps twenty seconds . . .

Liz You all right?

Vanessa Why shouldn't I be?

Eve We thought you might be ill.

Vanessa What gave you that idea.

Liz Judy said you seemed upset.

Eve Fraught.

Liz Yes, fraught.

Judy I didn't! I mean . . . that is—

Eve Under the weather.

Liz Off colour.

Vanessa There's nothing the matter with me.

Judy I never said there was! Oh, you two! Honestly, I could . . . Why do you do it?

Eve Do what?

Judy Twist things.

Liz Twist?

Judy Distort things, put words in my mouth!

Liz Well, if that's the way you feel—

Judy Yes, it is! That's exactly the way I feel and ... and I'm bloody sick of it! So now you know. (*Pause*) I don't know why I let you do it.

Eve It?

Judy It happens every time. Well, it won't happen again. I won't be provoked, I shall stay calm.

Liz Good.

Judy (*picking up sticks of greasepaint from table and putting them into the make-up box*) I mean it. Whatever you say, whatever either of you says, I shall ignore it. I'll be like one of those little Buddahs, completely calm, with a beautiful smile. From now on, nothing is going to make me ... (*She picks up the empty brandy glass. She stares at it, horrified*) Oh, no! (*She wheels round*) Who's had it?

Liz The brandy? (*She shrugs*) I had a tiny sip—

Judy Sip? Sip! It was a full glass!

Liz Well perhaps two tiny sips.

Judy A full glass!

Liz If you say so.

Vanessa, who has finished changing into her costume, crosses to the make-up table

Vanessa Excuse me, ladies. (*She sits and begins to make-up*)

Judy What do you think she's going to say?

Liz What do I think who's going to say?

Judy Irene. It was hers. She asked me to get her a brandy and soda, so I ran to the bar—

Eve I'll bet you did.

Judy —and ran back with it.

Liz Then why didn't she drink it?

Judy She went to look for Lesley. She put it down on the table and went upstairs. (*Pause*) Why did you drink it?

Liz I thought it was yours.

Judy I don't touch alcohol. It gives me a headache. Anyway, What gave you the right to take my brandy?

Liz It wasn't yours.

Judy But you thought it was! Oh, you are so selfish—

Liz Me? Selfish?

Judy Yes! You see a glass of brandy and you drink it. You don't stop to ask yourself if you have a right to it. Oh no! What Liz wants, Liz must have! (*Pause*) Oh God, I'm doing exactly what I said I wouldn't, I'm letting you provoke me. (*She struggles to control herself*) Well, I won't. I'm going to be completely calm. Nothing you say or do is going to provoke me. (*Pause*) Well, what have you got to say?

Pause

Liz (*quietly*) I'm sorry.

Judy What?

Liz You're right. I am selfish. (*She clasps Judy's hand and speaks with a throb in her voice*) Dear, dear Judy! Can you find it in your heart to forgive me?

Judy stares at her in disbelief, then snatches her hand away

Judy Oh, you ... bitch!

Liz and Eve fall about laughing
Irene enters UR

Irene I'm glad someone has something to laugh about. There's no sign of Lesley and we're twenty minutes from curtain.

Eve What do we do if she doesn't arrive?

Irene I shall go on and read the part.

Eve You? But—

Irene You don't have to say it. I don't make a very convincing twenty year old virgin.

Liz If it comes to that, neither does Lesley.

Irene Unkind. If true. (*Briskly*) However, we've no choice. The show must go on. We'll lose marks, of course, but at least we'll have preserved our honour.

Vanessa (*who has just completed her make-up*) Which is more than can be said for Lesley. (*She smiles sweetly at Irene in the mirror*) Sorry.

Irene Thank you. I want to go over the last couple of pages, from Donna Juana's entrance. (*She opens the script*)

Vanessa Now?

Irene Yes, now.

Vanessa But I haven't finished dressing.

Irene I had noticed. Perhaps you would. (*Pause*) Now.

Vanessa rises and stalks over to the costume rack. She snatches her black blouse from its hanger and starts to put it on

Good. Now, let's move these chairs. Judy . . .

Judy moves chairs and stools to wall R, *leaving middle of stage clear*

Right. I'll read Jacquetta. (*She stands* C) Laurencia . . .

Liz takes her position facing Irene

Vanessa I thought we were taking it from my entrance?
Irene We'll lead into it. Liz—
Liz Stay a moment, little sister.
Irene Out of my way—
Vanessa Would you like me to wear my wig?
Irene I don't care whether you wear it or not!
Vanessa Just so long as I know. (*She takes her wig from the block on the make-up table and puts it on during the next few speeches*)
Irene Again, Liz.
Liz Stay a moment, little sister . . .
Irene Out of my way.
Liz Not until you tell me where you've been, skulking round the courtyard like a thief.
Irene I'll scratch your eyes out!

They struggle, not very convincingly as Irene has the book in her hand

Liz Mother! Oh Mother!

Vanessa "enters"

Vanessa Silence! What is this noise which shatters the peace of the house?
Liz She's been with her lover! Look at the mud on her skirt. She's been with Don Estaban!
Vanessa Is this true? Daughter, answer me!

Noise of horses' hooves made by Judy with coconut shells

Liz There's your answer!

Eve "enters"

Eve Don Estaban has just ridden away! I recognized his piebald mare.

Vanessa Is this true? Is he your lover?
Irene Ask him yourself. If you can catch him!
Liz Thief!
Eve Whore!
Liz You're a disgrace to this house!
Irene You say that because you want him for yourself! Yes, both of you! You lust after him. But it's me he loves—me! And tomorrow he'll return and take me away!
Vanessa (*raising her hand*) Silence!
Irene Strike me! Go ahead. I don't care—

Judy strikes her hands together to produce musket shot. The others react

Vanessa What was that?

Everyone stares intently into audience. Judy shields her eyes with her hand

Judy I do believe . . .
Vanessa Yes. What can you see?
Judy Don Estaban has fallen from his horse!
Irene No!
Judy Yes! A passing brigand has brought him down with one shot from his musket. He's bending over him . . . I see a knife flash . . . He's cut his throat!

Irene howls with grief and "exits" L

Vanessa Daughter, come back! Where has she gone?
Judy To the courtyard. (*She tries imaginary door handle*) She's locked the door behind her!
Vanessa Don't think you can hide your shame! (*To Judy*) Knock the door down!

Judy takes several steps backward, then hurls herself at the imaginary door. Walks in. Runs on the spot. Pause. Screams

What is that terrible cry?

Judy "enters"

Judy God preserve us! (*She crosses herself*) She's—
Vanessa Yes?
Judy She's—

Liz
Eve } (*together*) Yes?

Judy She's thrown herself down the well!

Vanessa wails with grief, arms extended, face distorted

> The UR *door bursts open and Lesley staggers into the dressing-room. She is dressed in motor-cycle gear and clutches a crash helmet. She stumbles forward to* C, *where she stands swaying on her feet*

Eve Better late than never.

Lesley opens her mouth as if to reply, then is violently sick into her helmet

Pause

Vanessa Well, that's one way of making an entrance.

Black-out

Guitar music for twenty seconds. Lights up. Lesley is slumped in chair C. *Judy is kneeling by her, a plastic cup of coffee in her hand. Irene is pacing between* UR *door and* DR

Irene I refuse to believe that this is happening to me!

Judy Come on, lovely. Just sip. You'll feel better for it.

Irene In thirty years in the theatre I have never experienced such selfishness, such lack of consideration—

Lesley moans

Is she going to be sick again? If she is—

Judy I don't know.

Irene Do you know how long we have before curtain up? Five minutes!

Judy I know that.

Irene But does she? And if she does, does she care?

Judy (*lifting cup to Lesley's lips*) Just try a sip. Hot and sweet it is. Make a new woman of you.

Lesley jerks her head aside, spilling some of the coffee

Silly girl. Spilt it you have.

Irene advances on Lesley

Irene Lesley, I want you on your feet and into your costume. I want you in the wings ready for curtain-up. If you let me down, I swear—

Judy It's no use shouting at her!

Irene I beg your pardon?

Judy Can't you see she's not well? Ranting and raving won't help matters.

Irene How dare you speak to me like that.

Judy It's sympathy the poor girl needs. She's in shock.

Irene Shock! She's paralytic!

Judy She's had too much to drink, yes. But why?

Irene How should I know?

Judy Shouldn't we try to find out?

Irene I neither know nor care how she came to be in this state. All I know is—

Judy That curtain up is in five minutes and it looks as if you'll have to wave goodbye to your precious trophy. Well, there are more important things in life.

Irene Judy!

Judy Yes?

Irene You've never spoken to me like this before.

Judy Better late than never.

Irene What's that supposed to mean?

Judy Look, do you want this show to go on?

Irene It's got to go on!

Judy Then leave Lesley to me. We're not on until twenty minutes into the act, right?

Irene Yes, but—

Judy I'll sober her up, get her into her costume. I'll see she doesn't miss her entrance.

Irene If you fail—

Judy Fail? "But screw your courage to the sticking place and we'll not fail." Isn't that what they say?

Irene Oh, no!

Judy Sorry?

Irene You have just quoted from ... the Scottish Play!

Judy The Scot ... ? Oh, you mean "Mac—

Irene Don't say it! (*She grabs Judy by the arm*) Quickly, outside!

Judy Where?

Irene Into the corridor, turn round three times, anti-clockwise, spit and swear. (*Pause*) Well?

Judy No.

Irene What do you mean, no?

Judy If you want to behave like a whirling dervish, go ahead. I'm not going to.

Irene But I didn't break the taboo! Look, Judy, darling, everyone does it—Johnny, Larry, Dame Peggy—when they forget themselves.

Judy Turn round three times, spit and swear?

Irene Yes.

Judy Ah, but they're real actors. I can just about cross the stage without falling over the furniture. So I hardly think anything I say or do would make much difference one way or the other, do you?

Pause

Irene Well, I'll leave you to it.

Judy Good.

Irene turns to go, then remembers her drink, moves to table

Irene What happened to my brandy?

Judy Sorry?

Irene My brandy and soda. I distinctly remember leaving it here.

Judy Yes. (*Pause*) I drank it.

Irene But you don't drink.

Judy That's another first, then, isn't it?

Irene seems about to reply, thinks better of it and exits UR

As the door closes behind Irene, the loudspeaker crackles into life

Voice Testing, testing. (*High-pitched whistle*) The hall is filling up nicely: civic dignitaries and their lady wives in the front row and ... yes, the adjudicator has just slipped out of the bar and is taking his seat. The atmosphere is electric. Stay tuned to this frequency ...

Judy Stupid man! (*To Lesley*) What am I going to do with you?

Lesley stretches and sits up

Lesley You could get me a drink.

Judy You—

Lesley Don't say it! Remember, you're a devout Methodist.

Judy Baptist. You've been shamming.

Lesley I haven't. I've been sick as a dog. You must have noticed.

Judy We all noticed.

Lesley stands, rather groggily, crosses to the make-up table and squints into the mirror

Lesley I look like death. If I met me on a dark night, I'd wet myself. Sorry.

Judy Why? If I met you on a dark night, I'd wet myself.

Lesley laughs loudly, stops suddenly and clutches her stomach

Lesley Don't make me laugh, please. I'll throw up again.

Judy Sit down.

Lesley No, I—

Judy Sit!

Lesley returns to chair and collapses into it

I'm going to clean up, help you change and get you on stage, but before I do—

Lesley You'd like an explanation?

Judy It would be nice. (*Pause*) Well?

Lesley D'you think I could have—

Judy A drink? Definitely not.

Lesley A cigarette, then?

Judy Get on with it.

Lesley You're dead rotten, you are. Well, we'd been celebrating.

Judy Who's we?

Lesley Wayne and me.

Judy What was the occasion? (*Lesley looks blank*) What were you celebrating?

Lesley I'm not sure that's the word. Fact, the more I think of it—

Judy Lesley!

Lesley Sorry. Look, have you anything to eat? I've not touched a thing since breakfast and most of that—

Judy —finished up in your helmet. You don't have to remind me. I might have something.

Judy crosses to table, picks up handbag and roots around in it

Lesley I could eat anything!

Judy You might have to. (*She brings out chocolate*) Half a Kit Kat?

Lesley Great! (*She leaps from chair and almost snatches the* *chocolate from Judy's hand*) You've saved my life. (*She devours the chocolate, then licks her fingers and sighs*) That was marvellous! (*She burps*) Pardon!

Judy Right, let's have it. What exactly were you celebrating?

Lesley The results of the test.

Judy Test?

Lesley Yes. The clinic phoned it through this morning.

Judy You mean you're—

Lesley Pregnant. Yes. (*Pause*) You might say something.

Judy What would you like me to say?

Lesley Whatever you think's appropriate. Congratulations or you silly cow.

Judy Congratulations.

Lesley Thanks. Pity you've no more chocolate—now I'm eating for two.

Judy What does Wayne think about it?

Lesley Oh, he's over the moon. His trouble is he lacks confidence. He's not too clever.

Judy Not executive material?

Lesley He's been on so many schemes and courses, he must hold some kind of record. He was an apprentice once, a carpenter, but he only lasted a month.

Judy Why was that, then?

Lesley Kept on trying to put square pegs into round holes. (*Pause*) He says this is the first job he's managed to get right.

Judy Have you set the day?

Lesley looks blank

For the wedding?

Lesley I'm not marrying him!

Judy You're not?

Lesley No. Oh, I like him. He's fun—well, most of the time—but like I said he's . . . limited.

Judy What about the baby?

Lesley What about it?

Judy Lesley, you're not going to . . .

Lesley Of course I'm not! What a thing to suggest!

Judy I'm sorry. I meant—

Lesley I know what you meant. The thought never entered my head.

Judy Lesley, please—

Lesley I'll bring it—him, her—up myself. I know it won't be easy, but so what? I'll manage. (*She hugs Judy*) Let's forget about it, OK? You were going to help me change, right? How long do we have before we're on?

Judy Oh. (*She looks at her wristwatch*) Fifteen minutes. No, ten.

Lesley Then we'd better get our skates on. (*She sits at the make-up table and sorts through the make-up box*) I'll just slap on a base and some eye shadow.

Judy Better change first. Where's your costume?

Lesley In the holdall. (*She starts to clean her face*)

Judy (*looking round dressing-room*) Where is it?

Lesley Where's what?

Judy The holdall. I don't see it.

Lesley freezes, staring into mirror. Pause

Lesley (*in a whisper*) On the pillion.

Judy Pillion?

Lesley Of Wayne's bike. He brought me here.

Judy Where is he now?

Lesley In the pub.

Judy Which pub?

Lesley I don't know. How many pubs are there in (*Insert name of town where the play is being performed*)? (*She turns to face Judy*) He's picking me up after the show. He doesn't like drama.

Pause

Judy Pity. I've been feeling there's going to be rather a lot of it about.

Black-out. Five seconds pause. Over the loudspeaker we hear dialogue from the play onstage. Fifteen seconds into the extract the tape is speeded up and the volume increased. After twenty more seconds of gobbledegook it finishes abruptly. Lights up. The stage is empty. After a few seconds Eve enters UR. She crosses to table, sits and stares into mirror

Eve What are you laughing at? (*She grimaces at her reflection*) You know your trouble? You don't appreciate art. (*She sticks out her tongue*) Oh, you're ugly! You really are ugly. (*She picks* *up bottle of baby lotion and pours some into her hand)* If I had a face like yours, I'd do away with myself. I really would . . .

Liz enters to hear the last two lines

Liz 'ello, 'ello, 'ello! What's this then? Talking to ourselves, are we? Looking for a one way ticket to the funny farm?

Eve *(swinging round on stool)* You'll never believe this, but I've just had a terrible nightmare!

Liz You don't say?

Eve Shall I tell you about it?

Liz No, thank you.

Eve Right. It was like this. *(She stands)* I was in this room. It was very light, lights everywhere. I was dazzled. I couldn't move. All round me there were people, women, dressed in black, moaning, keening—

Liz Irish, were they?

Eve No, Spanish.

Liz Sorry. Carry on.

Eve They spoke to me. Asked questions. I couldn't understand a word. I shouted "I don't understand! Let me out!" *(She mimes her distress)* But they blocked my path, white faces thrust into mine, eyes rolling, hands clutching. I felt myself being dragged down, down, down . . . I shouted "I want to go home!"

Liz Yes?

Eve Then I woke up.

Liz Poor you!

Eve You know something?

Liz It wasn't a dream at all.

They both burst out laughing

Vanessa enters UR. She brushes past them to the costume rack and starts to change

They stop laughing. Eve winks at Liz and they go into their "Gert and Daisy" routine

Eve *(in broad cockney)* 'ere Daisy. Wot you think o' that, then?

Liz Wot do I think o' wot, Gert?

Eve All them women dressed in black, dashin' arand, weepin' an' wailin' an' beatin' their breasts?

Liz Ooh, I don't think you should say that, Gert!

Eve Say wot, Daisy?

Liz You know, Gert.

Eve I'm sure I don't, Daisy.

Liz That word, Gert.

Eve Wot word, Daisy?

Liz That word wot refers to a particular part of the female anatomy.

Eve You mean—

Liz Yes, Gert.

Eve Not in public, Daisy?

Liz Not when gentlemen are present, Gert.

Eve Wot gentleman?

Liz The three in the second row.

Eve They were asleep, Daisy.

Liz You sure, Gert?

Eve Either that or they were dead.

Liz That's all right then.

Vanessa Oh, very funny!

Eve I think she likes us, Daisy.

Liz D'you really think so, Gert?

Eve Oh I do, Daisy. I really think she likes us.

Liz What a lovely lady.

Eve And talented, too.

Liz A lovely mover.

Eve Poetry in motion. I could watch her for hours.

Vanessa That's enough!

Eve Sorry?

Vanessa You think you're so funny, don't you? After that . . . (*She gestures in direction of the stage*) farce, that humiliating exhibition out there, you can joke?

Liz What do you suggest we do, deary? Cut our throats?

Vanessa You've never taken this play seriously, either of you. As far as you're concerned it's been one big giggle from start to finish.

Eve (*in a refined Scottish accent*) Do I detect a note of disapprobation in what this lady's saying, sweetie?

Liz (*ditto*) I think you may be right. She sounds none too pleased.

Lesley enters UR. *She is still wearing her motor cycle gear. She ignores the other three women, crosses to the table, slumps onto a stool and buries her head in her arms*

Vanessa Happy? (*Pause*) Well, aren't you going to say something?

You've succeeded in ruining the play, eight weeks work up in smoke—

Judy has entered UR *in time to hear this*

Judy That's enough.
Vanessa I beg your pardon?
Judy Leave her alone. (*She sits beside Lesley, puts her arm round her shoulder*) She's had a hard time.
Vanessa That's rich! How do you think I feel?
Judy I don't know and to tell you the truth I don't much care. (*To Lesley*) Come on, lovely. It's not the end of the world.

Lesley bursts into tears

There now. It could have been worse.
Vanessa I suppose we should be grateful she didn't do a circuit of the auditorium on her bloody bike before knocking the adjudicator down!

Lesley wails even more loudly

Stupid girl!
Judy That's unfair!
Vanessa She ruined the performance.
Judy She's going through an emotional crisis.
Eve Tell us more.
Liz We're all ears.
Judy Shut up!
Eve Pardon us for breathing.
Judy Can't you see she's in a state of shock?
Vanessa I'm in a state of shock! I expected my daughter to enter from stage right and this ... refugee from the Manx TT staggered in from stage left. Is it any wonder I dried?

Irene enters UR

Everyone falls silent, apart from Lesley who still sobs convulsively. Irene moves C. *Long pause*

Irene You realise, of course, that we should all be out there awaiting the adjudicator's verdict.
Lesley Oh, no!
Irene My sentiments exactly. There are occasions when discretion is the better part of valour. This is one of them.

Lesley Oh Irene! I . . . I'm sorry—
Irene No apologies, please.
Lesley But I ruined the play!
Irene With a little help from your friends. No, don't say anything more. I'm feeling curiously calm, almost detached. No doubt when the numbness wears off I shall have something to say.
Lesley Oh my God!
Irene I suggest you all get changed as quickly as possible, then we'll steal off silently into the night.
Liz Oh well . . .

Liz, Eve and Vanessa begin to change. Judy remains at the table with her arm round Lesley

Lesley I wish I were dead!
Judy Don't be silly.
Lesley I do! I'd like to crawl away and die or . . . or drown myself or slash my wrists . . .
Irene I hope not. Otherwise we'll be in trouble with the caretaker as well as the adjudicator. Which reminds me. We might as well hear what the dear man has to say.

She moves UR *to loudspeaker*

Eve Do we have to?

Irene turns up volume control. Voice of the Adjudicator comes over in mid-sentence

Adjudicator . . . the third play in this week's festival by an all-women group. You'll remember that on Tuesday we had the Croxley Townswomen's Guild in "Little Women", a pleasant if not particularly memorable performance, and last night the Wheatsheaf Players gave us act one of "The Brontës of Haw-arth"—sixty-five minutes of Yorkshire gloom and doom, not including the unscheduled interval after the fireplace fell on Charlotte's foot—
Liz Nasty!
Adjudicator I was obliged to penalise them for overrunning.
Irene Oh dear.
Adjudicator Now we come to the Amazon Theatre Group's production of act three of "The Well of Defilement" by Juan

Ruiz de Aragon, a little known classic of seventeenth century Spanish drama ...

(From this point until the end of the play the reactions of the women on stage mirror the Adjudicator's words—indifference, slowly awakening interest, stunned disbelief at what they are hearing ...)

... this is a play of emotion and thwarted sexual passion. The cast must throw inhibition and restraint to the winds and show us the canker of hatred which eats at the heart of each of these women. *(Pause)* I must admit I had my doubts. Could a group of Englishwomen, however talented and well-rehearsed, get into the skins of Aragon's Spaniards? Such raw passion is foreign to our nature and we could so easily have been embarrassed—but we weren't. From the moment the curtain went up we were swept into their world, a world three hundred years old where casual sex is unheard of and if a young girl exchanges an unguarded word with a man she is considered either defiled or betrothed ... There were so many moments I shall treasure, the hatred in the voices and, even more, in the eyes of these women. This was acting of a very high order—

Liz and Eve, arms round each other, are shaking with silent laughter

But the thing which stamps this production as exceptional, which causes it to stand head and shoulders above anything we have seen this week, is the director's inspiration in having Jacquetta, the tragic heroine, wear motor-cycle gear—a masterstroke, symbolising her alienation from her family and her longing for freedom! All I can say is "Viva!"

Audience applause. Fade. Pause

Irene moves slowly C

Irene Darlings, you were wonderful!

Black-out

CURTAIN

FURNITURE AND PROPERTY LIST

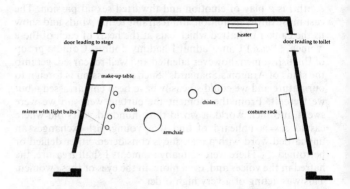

On stage: **Make-up table.** *On it:* make-up box, grey wig on a block,
                    aerosol, cloth, two coconut shells, ashtray, baby lotion
                    Chairs
                    Stools
                    Costume rack on castors. *On it:* 17th century Spanish costumes
                    Convector heater
                    Carpet
                    Pendant light with green lampshade

Off stage: Glass of brandy **(Judy)**
                    Script **(Irene)**
                    Plastic cup containing coffee **(Judy)**

Personal: **Vanessa:** large leather bag, magazine, cigarette
                    Irene: large antique ring, watch
                    Lesley: motor-cycle helmet
                    Judy: handbag. *In it:* half a bar of chocolate, watch

LIGHTING PLOT

To open: Black-out. After a few seconds lights up

Cue 1	**Judy:** "Butterflies, I suppose." *Fade lights. After twenty seconds lights up*	(Page 17)
Cue 2	**Vanessa:** "Well, that's one way of making an entrance" *Black-out. After twenty seconds lights up*	(Page 15)
Cue 3	**Judy:** ". . . rather a lot of it about." *Black-out*	(Page 20)
Cue 4	High-speed dialogue tape ends *Lights up*	(Page 20)
Cue 5	**Irene:** "Darlings, you were wonderful!" *Black-out*	(Page 25)

EFFECTS PLOT

To open: Classical Spanish guitar music

Cue 1   As lights come up   (Page 1)
           Music fades

Cue 2   **Judy:** "... What can we do without men?"   (Page 4)
           *Crackle of loudspeaker. Piercing whistle. Voice. More
               crackling*

Cue 3   **Judy:** "Butterflies, I suppose."   (Page 7)
           Guitar music for twenty seconds

Cue 4   **Vanessa:** "Well, that's one way of making an   (Page 15)
               entrance."
           Guitar music for twenty seconds

Cue 5   **Judy:** "That's another first then, isn't it?   (Page 17)
           Crackle of loudspeaker. Voice

Cue 6   **Judy:** "... rather a lot of it about." Five seconds   (Page 20)
               pause
           *Play on stage heard over loudspeaker for fifteen
               seconds. Speeded up to gobbledegook for twenty
               more seconds*

Cue 7   **Eve:** "Do we have to?"   (Page 24)
           Voice of adjudicator comes over loudspeaker

MADE AND PRINTED IN GREAT BRITAIN BY
LATIMER TREND & COMPANY LTD PLYMOUTH

MADE IN ENGLAND